AF656275

Sanjeev Kapoor

Cocktail Snacks

In association with Alyona Kapoor

Popular Prakashan
www.popularprakashan.com

Published by
POPULAR PRAKASHAN PVT. LTD.
301, Mahalaxmi Chambers
22, Bhulabhai Desai Road
Mumbai - 400 026
for Khana Khazana Publications Pvt. Ltd.

© 2011 Sanjeev Kapoor
First Published 2011
Second Reprint October 2015

WORLD RIGHTS RESERVED. The contents – all recipes, photographs and drawings are original and copyrighted. No portion of this book shall be reproduced, stored in a retrieval system or transmitted by any means, electronic, mechanical, photocopying, recording or otherwise, without the written permission of the author and the publisher.

(4423)
ISBN: 978-81-7991-675-9

Design: Anjali Sawant
Typesetting: Sanika Barje
Photography: Alim Bolar, Bharat Bhirangi, Mukesh Munim, Swapnil Nayak

PRINTED IN INDIA
by Saurabh Printers (P) Ltd.
Plot No. 67 A-68, Ecotech, Ext. I
Kasna, Greater Noida-201306 (U.P)

contents

Author's Note 5

Vegetarian

Achaari Pineapple Tikka 6
Hara Bhara Paneer Tikka 8
Cocktail Idli 11
Crunchy Paneer Pakore 13
Dahi ke Kabab 15
Mini Tostadas 17
Microwaved Kothimbir Wadi 21
Thread Paneer 22
Paneer Koliwada 24
Paneer Satay 25
Naughty 'N' Nice Nachos 27
Paneer and Peanut Samose 31
Momos 33
Mozzarella Skewers 35
Microwaved Cheesy Mushrooms 36
Mozzarella-Stuffed Chillies 37
Sago-Potato Rolls 38
Crispy Wontons 41
Khumb Shashlik 42
Corn and Vegetable Lollipops 43
Green Pea Potli 45
Makai, Badam aur Akhrot ki Tikki 47
Honeyed Potato Fingers 51
Lehsuni Paneer Tikka 52
Falafel 54
Corn Handvo 56

Non-Vegetarian

Crisp Chicken Baskets 58
Fish Cakes with Cucumber Relish 61

Fried Golden Bags 63
Fried Prawn Balls 65
Quick Canapés 66
Chicken Makhmali Kabab 68
Kali Mirch Tikka 71
Cheese Balls 73
Murgh ke Shami 74
Chicken Lollipops 76
Til Jhinga 77
Chao Tom 81
Keema Potli 83
Salsa Fresca 85

Dips
Thousand Island Dip 86
Roasted Capsicum and Tomato Dip 87
Crudités with Herbed Paneer and Yogurt Dip 88
Avocado Dip 89
Peanut Yogurt Dip 89
Cheese and Herb Dip 90
Saucy Tomato Dip 90
Melting Cheese Dip 91
Fish Sauce Dip 91

Basic Recipes
Mayonnaise 92
Red curry paste 92
Sichuan sauce 92
Vegetable stock 93
White sauce 93
Wonton wrappers 94

Glossary 95

author's note

Planning a cocktail party is easy! All you need is an interesting mix of people and a delectable spread of food. However, the hostess always worries about what cocktail snacks to serve when entertaining. To cater to different tastes and preferences, and most importantly, wow them with an array of tempting snacks is a challenge worth taking on.

My new collection of vegetarian and non-vegetarian cocktail snacks offers you a gamut of easy to make, lip smacking dishes that you can enjoy and impress your guests with. Try the tasty Cocktail Idli, melt in the mouth Kothimbir Wadi, luscious Dahi ke Kabab, bite size Mini Tostadas, irresistible Fried Prawns Balls, and light and red hot Mozzarella-Stuffed Chillies.

Throw a party worth remembering!

Happy Cooking!

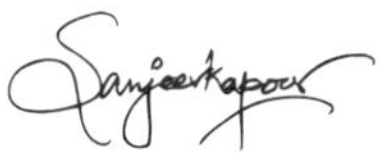

achaari pineapple tikka

5-6 tablespoons mango pickle

1 medium fresh pineapple

½ teaspoon onion seeds

½ teaspoon coriander seeds

¼ teaspoon fenugreek seeds

2 cups yogurt, drained

1 teaspoon ginger-garlic paste

½ teaspoon mustard powder

3 tablespoons oil

½ teaspoon turmeric powder

1 teaspoon *garam masala* powder

1 teaspoon red chilli powder

Salt to taste

Peel the pineapple and quarter it vertically. Remove the inner core and cut into one-inch thick slices.

Dry-roast the onion seeds, coriander seeds and fenugreek seeds. Cool and crush them coarsely.

Place the mango pickle in a bowl; remove the pieces of mango and use only the pickle *masala*.

Mix together the drained yogurt, pickle *masala*, roasted spice powder, ginger-garlic paste, mustard powder, oil, turmeric powder, *garam masala* powder, chilli powder and salt in a bowl. Marinate the pineapple in the mixture for fifteen minutes.

Preheat an oven to 180°C/350°F/Gas Mark 4.

Thread the pineapple pieces onto skewers and brush with the remaining marinade. Cook in the preheated oven for three to four minutes.

Serve with chutney.

hara bhara paneer tikka

300 grams cottage cheese, cut into 1½-inch cubes

2 bunches (120 grams) fresh coriander, roughly chopped

1 bunch (60 grams) fresh mint, roughly chopped

4 green chillies, roughly chopped

10 garlic cloves, roughly chopped

1 cup yogurt

3 tablespoons gram flour

Salt to taste

1 teaspoon *chaat masala*

½ teaspoon *garam masala* powder

1 tablespoon lemon juice

1 tablespoon oil

Coarsely grind the chopped coriander, mint, green chillies and garlic. Transfer to a bowl, add the yogurt, gram flour, salt, *chaat masala*, *garam masala* powder and lemon juice, and mix well.

Stir in the oil. Add the cottage cheese and mix well so that all the pieces are well-coated with the mixture. Set aside to marinate for about half an hour.

Heat a non-stick *tawa*. Thread the cottage cheese pieces one-inch apart onto skewers and grill, turning from time to time, for about fifteen minutes, or till evenly cooked on all sides. Serve hot with onion rings and lemon wedges.

cocktail idli

1 cup parboiled rice

½ cup skinless split black gram

Salt to taste

1 large onion, cut into 1-inch cubes, layers separated

1 large green capsicum, cut into 1-inch pieces

1 large tomato, seeded and cut into 1-inch pieces

2 tablespoons oil

2 tablespoons tomato ketchup

1 tablespoon red chilli sauce

12 toothpicks

Rasam, as required

Wash the rice and soak in three cups of water for at least two to three hours.

Wash and soak the split black gram in two cups of water for a similar length of time.

Drain and grind the rice to a slightly coarse texture. Add enough water to make a batter of dropping consistency.

Drain and grind the split black gram, sprinkling water as required to a make a smooth, spongy batter.

Mix both the batters together. Add salt and mix thoroughly in a whipping motion with your hand. Pour the batter into a large container, close tightly with a lid and leave to stand in a warm place overnight or for at least six hours.

Heat sufficient water in a steamer. Place a piece of wet muslin on the moulds of a mini *idli* stand. Pour a spoonful of the fermented batter into each mould. Place the *idli* stand in the steamer. Cook for eight to ten minutes or till the *idli* are done. Remove the *idli* from the moulds.

Thread the *idli* and vegetables onto each toothpick in the following order: onion, *idli*, capsicum, *idli*, tomato. Heat the oil in a non-stick pan and arrange the skewered *idli* on it. Add the tomato ketchup and chilli sauce, and toss to coat the *idli* with the sauce.

Serve the *idli* with the *rasam*. Pour a little *rasam* into small glasses, place the toothpicks across the rims. Serve immediately.

Chef's Tip

If you do not have mini *idli* moulds, you can make the *idli* in the normal size and cut into quarters.

crunchy paneer pakore

250 grams cottage cheese

Oil for deep-frying

1 cup *boondi*

Garlic Chutney

8-10 garlic cloves

1 teaspoon oil

2 teaspoons red chilli powder

Salt to taste

Batter

1 cup gram flour

1½ inches ginger

5 garlic cloves

½ teaspoon red chilli powder

½ teaspoon turmeric powder

A pinch of soda bicarbonate

Salt to taste

Wash and cut the cottage cheese into two-inch by half-inch by half-inch pieces. Slit each piece in half leaving one edge intact for filling.

Crush the *boondi* with your hand and set aside.

To make the garlic chutney, peel and roast the garlic in one teaspoon of oil. Mix with the chilli powder and salt and grind to a smooth paste.

To prepare the batter, grind together the ginger and garlic to a paste. Mix the gram flour with the paste, chilli powder, turmeric powder, soda bicarbonate and salt.

Add sufficient water and whisk well to make a batter of coating consistency. Rest the batter for about fifteen minutes.

Stuff the garlic chutney into the slit in each piece of cottage cheese.

Heat sufficient oil in a non-stick *kadai*; dip each piece of cottage cheese into the batter, roll in the crushed *boondi* and deep-fry on medium heat till crisp and golden brown.

Serve hot with tomato ketchup or Green Chutney (see below).

Green Chutney

Grind together 1 cup fresh coriander, ½ cup fresh mint, 2-3 green chillies, black salt to taste, ¼ teaspoon sugar and 1 tablespoon lemon juice to a smooth paste using a little water if required.

dahi ke kabab

½ cup drained (hung) yogurt

5 French beans, boiled and mashed

½ cup shelled green peas, boiled and mashed

9 small potatoes, boiled, peeled and mashed

2 tablespoons oil + for deep-frying

1 inch ginger, chopped

2 green chillies, chopped

1 teaspoon *garam masala* powder

1½ tablespoons chopped fresh coriander

Salt to taste

2½ tablespoons cornflour

1 cup breadcrumbs

Heat two tablespoons of oil in a non-stick pan on medium heat; add the ginger and green chillies, and sauté for a minute.

Add the French bean paste and green pea paste and sauté for two minutes.

Add the potatoes, *garam masala* powder, coriander and salt. Mix well, and set aside to cool.

Add the cornflour and mix well. Divide into eight equal portions and shape into balls.

Divide the drained yogurt into eight equal portions. Moisten your palms and place one portion of the potato mixture on a palm, and gently spread out into a small disc.

Place one portion of the yogurt in the centre, bring in the edges together and seal, ensuring that the yogurt is completely covered with the potato mixture. Roll into a ball and press lightly.

Roll the kababs in the breadcrumbs till they are covered all around.

Heat sufficient oil in a non-stick *kadai*. Add the kababs, a few at a time, and deep-fry on medium heat till evenly browned. Drain on an absorbent paper.

Serve hot with chutney.

mini tostadas

12 ready-made corn tostadas

A few iceberg lettuce leaves, torn into bite-size pieces

1 tablespoon pomegranate kernels

A few sprigs of fresh parsley

Salsa

½ cup sweetcorn kernels

1 tablespoon olive oil

1 medium onion, chopped

1 medium green capsicum, cut into small pieces

1 medium red capsicum, cut into small pieces

1 medium yellow capsicum, cut into small pieces

50 grams cottage cheese, cut into small pieces

7-8 black peppercorns, crushed

¼ teaspoon paprika

1 tablespoon chopped fresh coriander

Salt to taste

1 tablespoon lemon juice

1 tablespoon balsamic vinegar (optional)

For the salsa, roast the corn in a non-stick pan over high heat to scorch the kernels lightly. Add the olive oil and onion, and sauté till translucent. Remove from heat and transfer to a bowl. Set aside to cool.

Place the capsicums and cottage cheese in a separate bowl. Add the crushed peppercorns, paprika, fresh coriander, salt and lemon juice, and mix well.

Add the sautéed corn and balsamic vinegar. Adjust salt and toss to mix.

To assemble, place the tostadas on a plate and place a piece of lettuce leaf on each one. Spoon some salsa on each tostada.

Garnish with pomegranate kernels and parsley sprigs, and serve immediately.

Chef's Tip

Ready-made tostadas are available in most grocery stores or supermarkets.

microwaved kothimbir wadi

2 cups fresh coriander, chopped

1 cup gram flour

Salt to taste

½ teaspoon turmeric powder

1 tablespoon red chilli powder

1 tablespoon ginger paste

1 tablespoon garlic paste

2 teaspoons grated jaggery

1 tablespoon tamarind pulp

½ teaspoon soda bicarbonate

2 tablespoons sesame seeds

3 tablespoons oil

½ teaspoon mustard seeds

8-10 curry leaves

In a bowl, mix together fresh coriander, gram flour, salt, turmeric powder, chilli powder, ginger paste, garlic paste, jaggery, tamarind pulp, soda bicarbonate and half the sesame seeds. Whisk in enough water to make a moderately thick, smooth batter.

Pour the batter into a greased six-inch square and one-and-a-half-inch deep microwave-safe tray. Sprinkle with the remaining sesame seeds.

Pour water into another microwave-safe tray that is larger in size than the previous one, and rest the tray with the batter in it. Cook, covered, on HIGH (100%) for ten minutes, or till firm and a skewer inserted into the *wadi* comes out clean.

Put the oil into a small microwave-safe bowl; add mustard seeds and curry leaves. Cook, uncovered, for two minutes on HIGH (100%), or till the seeds start to splutter. Pour over the *wadi* and serve immediately.

thread paneer

250 grams cottage cheese

6 garlic cloves, chopped

2 tablespoons sweet chilli sauce

2 tablespoons lemon juice

1 teaspoon white pepper powder

¼ teaspoon MSG (optional)

1 tablespoon soy sauce

2 teaspoons sugar

Salt to taste

2 tablespoons refined flour

1 tablespoon cornflour

6 spring roll wrappers, cut into thin strips

Oil for deep-frying

Cut the cottage cheese into two-inch long, half-inch wide and half-inch thick fingers.

In a bowl, mix together the garlic, sweet chilli sauce, lemon juice, white pepper powder, MSG, soy sauce, sugar and salt. Apply this mixture liberally on the cottage cheese fingers and set aside to marinate for fifteen minutes.

Mix together the refined flour and cornflour, and add to the cottage cheese mixture. Mix well. Set aside for ten minutes. Spread the spring roll wrapper strips in a plate. Roll the marinated cottage cheese in them. Press well with your hand so that the strips stick to the cottage cheese.

Heat sufficient oil in a non-stick wok, deep-fry the cottage cheese fingers for two to three minutes on medium heat, turning frequently or until crisp and golden brown in colour. Drain on an absorbent paper. Serve hot with a sauce of your choice.

paneer koliwada

300 grams cottage cheese
½ cup gram flour
½ teaspoon cumin powder
2 teaspoons Kashmiri red chilli powder
Salt to taste
1 tablespoon ginger paste
1 tablespoon garlic paste
2 tablespoons yogurt
2 tablespoons lemon juice
Oil for deep-frying
½ teaspoon *chaat masala*

Chef's Tip

To make Paneer Koliwada extra crisp, add a tablespoon of cornflour to the batter.

Cut the cottage cheese into three-inch by half-inch by half-inch pieces.

Mix together the gram flour, cumin powder, chilli powder, salt, ginger paste, garlic paste, yogurt, lemon juice and a little water if necessary, into a thick batter.

Marinate the cottage cheese in the batter for half an hour. Heat the oil in a non-stick *kadai* and deep-fry the cottage cheese till crisp on the outside.

Serve hot, sprinkled with *chaat masala*.

paneer satay

500 grams cottage cheese, cut into 2-inch thick fingers

Salt to taste

2 tablespoons soy sauce

1 teaspoon lemon juice

4 garlic cloves, crushed

1 inch ginger, crushed

2 teaspoons brown sugar

2 teaspoons honey

Oil for basting

Peanut Sauce

1 tablespoon oil

1 small onion, chopped

½ inch ginger, crushed

4 garlic cloves, crushed

1 tablespoon soy sauce

6 tablespoons peanut butter

4 tablespoons Coconut Milk (see below)

1 tablespoon lemon juice

Salt to taste

1 tablespoon honey

1 fresh red chilli, seeded and chopped

Place the cottage cheese fingers in a bowl. Add the salt, soy sauce, lemon juice, garlic, ginger, brown sugar and honey, and mix. Marinate for one hour preferably in a refrigerator.

Heat the oil in a non-stick griddle or *tawa*. Thread the marinated cottage cheese onto satay sticks and place on the griddle. Pour some of the excess marinade over the cottage cheese and cook, turning the satay sticks to brown the cottage cheese evenly on all sides.

For the peanut sauce, heat the oil in a non-stick pan; add the onion and sauté for a few minutes. Add the ginger and garlic, and continue to sauté. Add the soy sauce, peanut butter and two tablespoons of water.

Stir in the coconut milk, lemon juice, salt and honey. Add the chopped red chilli and remove from heat. Serve the satay with the sauce.

Coconut Milk

Process 1 cup grated fresh coconut in a blender with ¼ cup warm water. Pass the ground coconut through a piece of muslin or strainer pressing firmly to extract all the juice, or first milk. Add a ¼ cup of warm water to the strained coconut to get the second, thinner milk from the same solids.

naughty 'n' nice nachos (nachos with cheese sauce and salsa)

¼ cup maize flour

¼ cup refined flour + for dusting

1 teaspoon oil + for deep-frying

Salt to taste

Cheese Sauce

½ cup grated processed cheese

1 tablespoon oil

6-8 garlic cloves, crushed

½ cup White Sauce (page 93)

½ teaspoon white pepper powder

Salsa

5 medium tomatoes, halved

1 tablespoon oil

2 onions, chopped

1 green chilli, chopped

1 teaspoon vinegar

Salt to taste

¼ teaspoon black pepper powder

2 tablespoons chopped fresh coriander

Mix together the maize flour, refined flour, one teaspoon oil and salt in a bowl. Add sufficient hot water and knead into a soft dough.

Divide the dough into six equal portions and roll into balls. Dust the balls with flour and roll out into thin *chapati*. Cut each *chapati* into four triangles.

Heat sufficient oil in a deep non-stick pan and deep-fry the triangles on low heat till crisp. Drain on absorbent paper and set aside to cool. To prepare the cheese sauce, heat the oil in a non-stick pan. Add the garlic and sauté for a few seconds. Stir in the white sauce, add the white pepper powder and cheese, and stir to mix.

For the salsa, heat a non-stick pan and roast the tomatoes till the skins char. Cool and peel. Chop two tomatoes and purée the rest. Heat the oil in a non-stick pan and sauté the onion and green chilli for two minutes.

Add the tomatoes, tomato purée, vinegar, salt and pepper powder, and cook for two minutes. Take the pan off the heat and set aside to cool. Stir in the chopped coriander.

To serve, arrange the tortilla chips on a plate, spread a little cheese sauce over them and top with the salsa. Serve immediately.

Chef's Tip

For a quicker, colourful topping, instead of the salsa, sprinkle finely chopped green, red and yellow capsicums on top of the cheese sauce.

paneer and peanut samose

Pastry

1½ cups refined flour + for dusting

Salt to taste

½ teaspoon carom seeds

6 tablespoons warm ghee

Oil for deep-frying

Filling

600 grams cottage cheese, grated

¼ cup peanuts, coarsely crushed

2 tablespoons oil

1 teaspoon cumin seeds

1 medium onion, chopped

3-4 green chillies, chopped

1 inch ginger, chopped

2 tablespoons raisins

Salt to taste

1½ teaspoons red chilli powder

2 tablespoons chopped fresh coriander

2 teaspoons chaat *masala*

For the pastry, sift the refined flour with salt into a large bowl. Add the carom seeds, warm ghee and one-fourth cup plus two tablespoons of water and knead to a stiff dough. Cover with a damp cloth and set aside for fifteen minutes.

To make the filling, heat the oil in a non-stick pan; add the cumin seeds and when they begin to change colour add the onion and sauté over medium heat for two minutes. Add the green chillies and ginger, and continue to sauté for another minute.

Add the peanuts, raisins, salt, chilli powder, chopped coriander and *chaat masala*, and cook for two minutes, stirring and tossing continuously.

Add grated cottage cheese, toss to mix well and transfer the mixture to a plate to cool.

To make the *samosa*, divide the dough into four equal portions and roll into balls. Sprinkle a little flour and roll out into four-inch wide ovals.

Cut each oval into half and brush the edges with water. Shape each half into a cone and stuff it with the filling. Press the edges together well to seal.

Heat oil in a non-stick *kadai* and deep-fry *samose*, two at a time, in medium hot oil till crisp and golden brown. Drain on absorbent paper.

Serve hot.

momos

1 cup refined flour

10 French beans, finely chopped

1 medium carrot, finely chopped

4-5 fresh button mushrooms, finely chopped

2 spring onions, finely chopped

¼ cup bean sprouts

8-10 cashew nuts, chopped

1 inch ginger, finely chopped

1 green chilli, finely chopped

8-10 black peppercorns, crushed

½ tablespoon light soy sauce

1 teaspoon sesame oil

¼ teaspoon MSG (optional)

Salt to taste

1 spring onion green, chopped

Mix the refined flour with five tablespoons of water and knead into a stiff dough. Cover with a damp cloth and set aside for fifteen minutes.

For the filling, in a large bowl, combine the French beans, carrot, mushrooms, spring onions, bean sprouts, cashew nuts, ginger, green chilli, peppercorns, soy sauce, sesame oil, MSG and salt to taste.

Divide the dough into sixteen equal portions and roll out into small thin discs.

Place a spoonful of the vegetable filling in the centre of each disc and bring the sides together in the centre, pinching firmly together to form a dumpling.

Line a steamer rack with a clean, damp piece of muslin and arrange the momos on it. Place the rack in the steamer, cover and steam for eight to ten minutes, until the momos are cooked through.

Transfer to a serving plate. Garnish with spring onion greens and serve hot with Sichuan Sauce (page 92).

mozzarella skewers

12 half-inch thick slices white bread

3 tablespoons olive oil

225 grams mozzarella cheese, cut into ¼-inch slices

3 medium tomatoes, cut into ¼-inch slices

20-25 fresh basil leaves

Salt to taste

10-12 black peppercorns, freshly ground

Preheat an oven to 220⁰C/425⁰F/Gas Mark 7.

Trim the bread crusts and cut each slice into four equal squares. Brush both sides with olive oil, arrange on a baking tray and bake for three to five minutes, or until the squares are pale gold. Remove from the oven. Thread stacks onto sixteen wooden skewers, starting each with a square of bread, followed by a slice of mozzarella, a slice of tomato and a basil leaf.

Sprinkle with salt and crushed peppercorns, and repeat the sequence ending with a slice of bread. Place the skewers on a baking tray and drizzle with remaining oil. Bake for ten to fifteen minutes or till the cheese begins to melt. Serve hot, garnished with fresh basil leaves.

Chef's Tip

Soak wooden skewers (satay sticks) in water for fifteen minutes to prevent them from charring.

microwaved cheesy mushrooms

16 medium-sized fresh button mushrooms

¼ cup crumbled cottage cheese

¼ cup grated processed cheese

1 medium onion, finely chopped

4-5 garlic cloves, finely chopped

¼ teaspoon white pepper powder

¼ teaspoon nutmeg powder

Salt to taste

5 tablespoons butter

1 tablespoon lemon juice

Remove the stalks of the mushrooms and chop finely.

Place chopped mushroom stalks, onion, garlic, cottage cheese, processed cheese, white pepper powder, nutmeg powder and salt in a microwave-safe dish. Add two tablespoons of butter and mix well.

Cook, uncovered, on HIGH (100%) for six minutes. Stuff the mushroom caps with the mixture; sandwich two caps together, holding them in place with a toothpick.

Brush the remaining butter and lemon juice over the mushrooms and cook, uncovered, on MEDIUM (70%) for three minutes. Serve hot with a spicy sauce.

mozzarella-stuffed chillies

8 Bhavnagri chillies, slit and seeded

8 pickled jalapeño chillies, slit and seeded

1 cup grated mozzarella cheese

2 teaspoons dried mixed herbs

1 cup cornflour

Salt to taste

2 cups fresh breadcrumbs

Oil for deep-frying

Mix the grated cheese and dried mixed herbs in a bowl. Stuff the mixture into the chillies.

Mix the cornflour, salt and two-third cup of water to make a batter.

Dip the chillies in the batter and roll them in the breadcrumbs. Repeat the process to get a double coating.

Heat the oil in a deep non-stick *kadai* till very hot and deep-fry the chillies till golden brown. Drain on absorbent paper. Serve hot.

sago-potato rolls

¾ cup sago

3 large potatoes, boiled and mashed

½ cup roasted and peeled peanuts, crushed

3 green chillies, chopped

1 inch ginger, chopped

1 tablespoon lemon juice

2-3 tablespoons chopped fresh coriander

Salt to taste

Oil for deep-frying

To Serve

Green Chutney (page 14)

Wash the sago and soak in water for at least one hour. If in a hurry, soak the sago in hot water till they swell. Squeeze out and place in a large bowl.

Add the potatoes, peanuts, green chillies, ginger, lemon juice, fresh coriander and salt and mix well. Add a little water if necessary and make a dough. Leave to stand for a few minutes. Divide the dough into eight equal portions and shape into oval rolls.

Heat sufficient oil in a non-stick *kadai* till medium hot. Slide in four rolls at a time and deep-fry till golden. Drain on absorbent paper. Serve hot with green chutney.

crispy wontons

24 Wonton Wrappers (page 94)

2 tablespoons oil + for deep-frying

4-6 garlic cloves, finely chopped

2 spring onions, finely chopped

2 medium green capsicums, finely chopped

8-10 French beans, finely chopped

2 medium carrots, finely chopped

½ small cabbage, finely chopped

½ teaspoon white pepper powder

Salt to taste

¼ teaspoon MSG (optional)

1 teaspoon light soy sauce

Heat two tablespoons of oil in a non-stick wok or pan; add the garlic and stir-fry for half a minute. Add the spring onions, green capsicums, French beans, carrots and cabbage, and continue to stir-fry for a couple of minutes more, stirring and tossing continuously. Add the white pepper powder, salt, MSG and soy sauce, and cook for half a minute. Take the pan off the heat and allow the vegetables to cool.

Divide the prepared filling into twenty-four equal portions. Place a portion of filling in the centre of each wonton wrapper; moisten the edges with a little water, fold in half diagonally, twist the ends and press lightly to stick together. Heat sufficient oil in a non-stick wok and deep-fry the wontons for two to three minutes, or until crisp and golden brown. Drain on absorbent paper. Serve hot with Sichuan Sauce (page 92).

khumb shashlik

10-12 large fresh button mushrooms

2 medium onions, cut into 1½-inch pieces

2 medium tomatoes, seeded and cut into 1½-inch pieces

2 medium green capsicums, seeded and cut into 1½-inch pieces

½ cup drained (hung) yogurt

2 teaspoons ginger-garlic paste

Salt to taste

½ tablespoon Kashmiri chilli powder

1 teaspoon *garam masala* powder

1 teaspoon crushed dried fenugreek leaves

4 teaspoons lemon juice

4 teaspoons oil

Chef's Tip

You can also cook the shashlik on a non-stick *tawa* for ten minutes till done; or in a preheated oven at 200°C/400°F/Gas Mark 6 for about 10 minutes.

Clean the mushrooms and remove the stems.

In a bowl, mix together the drained yogurt, ginger-garlic paste, salt, chilli powder, *garam masala* powder, crushed dried fenugreek leaves, lemon juice and oil.

Add the mushrooms, onions, tomatoes and capsicums, and mix. Set aside to marinate for thirty minutes. Thread the marinated vegetables onto skewers in the following order: mushroom, onion, tomato and capsicum; repeat once. Grill for six to eight minutes.

Serve hot with Green Chutney (page 14), onion rings and lemon wedges.

corn and vegetable lollipops

½ cup fresh corn kernels, crushed
16 pieces baby corn
1 medium carrot, finely chopped
¼ cup shelled green peas, crushed
2 large potatoes, boiled and mashed
1 tablespoon oil + for deep-frying
Salt to taste
1 inch ginger, chopped
4-6 garlic cloves, chopped
2-3 green chillies, chopped
1 medium onion, chopped
1 tablespoon fresh coriander, chopped
½ tablespoon light soy sauce
½ teaspoon white pepper powder
¼ teaspoon MSG (optional)
2 tablespoons cornflour
¼ cup refined flour

Heat one tablespoon of oil in a non-stick pan.

Add the carrot and peas, and sauté for a few seconds. Add the crushed corn and salt, and cook till the vegetables soften slightly.

Place the mashed potatoes in a bowl; add the sautéed vegetables, ginger, garlic, green chillies, onion, chopped coriander, soy sauce, white pepper powder, MSG, salt and cornflour. Mix thoroughly.

Divide the mixture into sixteen equal portions. Roll each portion into a ball and insert the thicker end of the baby corn into the ball. Press the mixture lightly between your palms to secure the baby corn.

Heat the oil in a non-stick wok; roll the lollipops in flour and shake to remove excess flour. Deep-fry over medium heat for three to four minutes, or till crisp and golden brown, turning occasionally. Drain on absorbent paper.

Serve hot with Sichuan Sauce (page 92).

green pea potli

1½ cups refined flour

Salt to taste

2 tablespoons ghee

Oil for deep-frying

Filling

1 cup shelled green peas, crushed

2 tablespoons oil

1 small onion, peeled and finely chopped

Salt to taste

1 teaspoon red chilli powder

½ teaspoon *garam masala* powder

2 tablespoons fresh coriander, finely chopped

¼ cup grated cheese

For the filling, heat two tablespoons of oil in a non-stick pan. Add the onion and sauté on high heat. When the onion become translucent, add the crushed peas and salt. Mix and cook for three to four minutes.

Add the chilli powder and *garam masala* powder and mix. Sauté for two minutes and transfer the mixture to a plate. Add the chopped coriander, mix and set aside to cool.

Sift the refined flour with salt. Add the ghee and enough water to make a stiff dough. Divide the dough into twelve equal portions and roll into balls. Flatten each ball slightly and roll out into a small disc.

Place the disc in your palm, moisten with a little water and place a portion of the filling in the centre. Add the grated cheese. Pleat the edges and gather the folds together, twisting slightly to make a *potli*.

Heat the oil in a non-stick *kadai* and deep-fry the *potli* till golden. Drain on absorbent paper and serve hot.

makai, badam aur akhrot ki tikki

1½ cups (300 grams) corn kernels, boiled and ground

20 almonds, blanched, peeled and ground

16 walnut halves, chopped

200 grams lotus roots

2 tablespoons oil + for shallow-frying

1 teaspoon caraway seeds

1 teaspoon red chilli powder

1 teaspoon black pepper powder

1 teaspoon fennel powder

1 teaspoon *garam masala* powder

1 teaspoon *chaat masala*

100 grams cottage cheese, grated

Salt to taste

½ cup grated processed cheese

1 tablespoon lemon juice

1 inch ginger, chopped

2 tablespoons chopped fresh coriander

24 raisins, chopped

Clean and scrape the lotus roots. Grate and boil until soft. Drain, squeeze out excess water and grind to a paste.

Heat two tablespoons of oil in a non-stick *kadai*; add the caraway seeds and sauté till fragrant.

Add the corn paste, almond paste and lotus root paste, and sauté till the moisture evaporates and the mixture is dry.

Add the chilli powder, pepper powder, fennel powder, *garam masala* powder and *chaat masala*, and mix well. Add the cottage cheese and salt, and stir to mix. Cook till the mixture thickens and the oil separates.

Remove from heat and stir in the processed cheese, lemon juice, ginger and chopped coriander. Set aside to cool.

Divide the cooled mixture into twenty equal balls. Stuff the balls with walnuts and raisins and shape into *tikki.*

Heat a little oil in a non-stick frying pan and shallow-fry the *tikki* on both sides. Drain on absorbent paper. Serve hot with Green Chutney (page 14)

honeyed potato fingers

4 large potatoes, peeled and cut into thin fingers

4 tablespoons honey

½ cup cornflour

2 tablespoons oil + for deep-frying

2 garlic cloves, crushed

2 tablespoons light soy sauce

2 tablespoons hoisin sauce

2 tablespoons red chilli flakes

Salt to taste

1 teaspoon lemon juice

1 tablespoon toasted sesame seeds

Mix two tablespoons of cornflour in one cup of water.

Heat sufficient oil in a non-stick wok or pan; dust the potato fingers with the remaining cornflour and deep-fry, turning frequently, for about four to five minutes. Drain on absorbent paper.

Heat two tablespoons of oil in a separate non-stick wok or pan; add the garlic and stir-fry for a few seconds. Stir in the soy sauce, hoisin sauce, red chilli flakes and salt to taste.

Add the fried potato fingers and stir in the cornflour mixture. Cook on medium to high heat for one minute, stirring continuously.

Lower the heat and stir in the lemon juice and honey. Mix well and cook on medium heat for a couple of minutes. Serve hot, sprinkled with toasted sesame seeds.

lehsuni paneer tikka

850 grams cottage cheese, cut into 1½-inch cubes

2 tablespoons garlic paste

2 tablespoons *tandoori masala*

300 grams drained (hung) yogurt

3½ tablespoons fresh cream

5-6 garlic cloves, chopped

1 green chilli, chopped

2 tablespoons chopped fresh coriander

Salt to taste

1 tablespoon red chilli powder

½ tablespoon turmeric powder

1½ tablespoons *garam masala* powder

1 tablespoon carom seed powder

1 tablespoon *chaat masala*

4 tablespoons roasted gram flour

1 tablespoon vinegar

2 tablespoons oil

Slit the cottage cheese cubes without cutting through.

Mix one tablespoon of the garlic paste and *tandoori masala* in a small bowl. Stuff the mixture into the slit cottage cheese cubes with your fingers. Set aside.

Mix together the yogurt, cream, remaining garlic paste, the chopped garlic, green chilli, fresh coriander, salt, chilli powder, turmeric powder, *garam masala* powder, carom seed powder, *chaat masala*, roasted gram flour, vinegar and oil in a bowl.

Soak the stuffed cottage cheese cubes in this marinade and set aside for around two hours in a refrigerator.

Preheat an oven to 200°C/400°F/Gas Mark 6.

Thread the cottage cheese cubes one inch apart onto skewers.

Cook the cottage cheese in the preheated oven for eight to ten minutes, or roast or grill over live charcoals, or in a *tandoor* over a moderate heat for six to eight minutes.

Serve hot with salad and Green Chutney (page 14).

falafel

1 cup chickpeas

2 tablespoons chopped parsley

2 tablespoons chopped fresh coriander

4-5 spring onion greens, chopped

2-3 garlic cloves, chopped

¼ cup breadcrumbs

A small pinch of soda bicarbonate

½ teaspoon cumin powder

Salt to taste

¼ teaspoon pepper powder

½ teaspoon paprika

Oil for deep-frying

Wash and soak the chickpeas overnight. Drain and dry on a kitchen towel.

In a food processor or blender, grind the chickpeas, parsley, chopped coriander, spring onion greens, garlic and breadcrumbs to a coarse mixture.

Add the soda bicarbonate and cumin powder, and mix well. Season with salt, pepper and paprika. Knead the mixture well and allow it to rest for a couple of hours in a refrigerator.

Place small quantities of the mixture in a tablespoon moistened with water and shape with the help of another moistened tablespoon to make smooth oval falafels.

Heat sufficient oil in a non-stick *kadai* and deep-fry the falafels till golden brown. Drain on absorbent paper and serve hot.

Chef's Tip

Falafel are traditionally served with tabbouleh and a tahina dip. Falafel are traditionally made with fava beans but you can use chickpeas instead. They can be shaped and stored on a greased plate in a refrigerator prior to frying.

corn handvo

1 cup crushed sweetcorn kernels
1 cup rice
½ cup split pigeon peas
¼ cup skinless split green gram
2 tablespoons split Bengal gram
2 tablespoons skinless split black gram
½ cup sour yogurt
2 teaspoons soda bicarbonate
Salt to taste
4 teaspoons sugar
2 teaspoons red chilli powder
¼ teaspoon turmeric powder
1 large onion, chopped
2 tablespoons chopped fresh coriander
2-3 green chillies, chopped
4 tablespoons oil
2 dried red chillies, broken in half
1 bay leaf
A pinch of asafoetida
1 teaspoon mustard seeds
1 tablespoon lemon juice

Soak the rice with all the lentils in five cups of water for two hours. Drain. Grind to a coarse paste and add enough water to make a moderately thick batter. Mix in the yogurt and one teaspoon of soda bicarbonate. Cover the batter and leave in a dark place for two to three hours to ferment.

Add the corn, salt, sugar, chilli powder, turmeric powder, onion, chopped coriander and green chillies to the batter and mix well.

Preheat an oven to 200°C/400°F/Gas Mark 6.

Heat the oil in a non-stick pan; sauté the red chillies, bay leaf, asafoetida and mustard seeds. Sprinkle the remaining soda bicarbonate over the batter and pour in the lemon juice. Immediately pour the hot seasoning over the batter and whisk briskly to mix.

Grease a baking tray. Pour the batter into it till half full.

Pour some water into a slightly larger baking tray and place the tray with the batter in it. Bake for twenty to twenty-five minutes.

Cut into wedges and serve hot.

crisp chicken baskets

2 (150 grams each) boneless chicken breasts, boiled and chopped

20 ready-made canapé cases

2 tablespoons butter

3 garlic cloves, chopped

2 medium onions, chopped

¼ cup White Sauce (page 93)

2 tablespoons grated processed cheese

Salt to taste

2 teaspoons black pepper powder

Grill the canapé shells in the grill mode of a microwave oven for three to five minutes, or until crisp and golden brown. Set aside.

Heat the butter in a non-stick pan; add the garlic and onions, and sauté for two to three minutes. Add the chicken and sauté for another two minutes.

Add the white sauce and cook for two minutes. Add the cheese, salt and pepper, and mix well. Set aside to cool slightly.

Fill the canapé shells with the chicken mixture and serve immediately.

fish cakes with cucumber relish

4 (300 grams) white fish fillets, cut into chunks

Salt to taste

2 tablespoons Red Curry Paste (page 92)

1 egg

1 tablespoon fish sauce

1 teaspoon sugar

3 tablespoons cornflour

1 tablespoon chopped fresh coriander

10-12 French beans, chopped and blanched

3 tablespoons breadcrumbs + to coat

Oil for deep-frying

Cucumber Relish

1 medium cucumber, quartered and sliced

4 tablespoons rice vinegar

1 tablespoon sugar

2 garlic cloves, chopped

4 shallots, sliced

1½ inches ginger, chopped

To make the cucumber relish, boil together the rice vinegar, two tablespoons water and the sugar in a non-stick pan.

Stir until the sugar dissolves, remove from the heat and cool. Mix the cucumber, garlic, shallots and ginger in a bowl and pour the vinegar mixture over it.

Boil the fish in salted water, drain thoroughly and cool.

Place the red curry paste, fish and egg in a food processor and blend well. Transfer the mixture to a bowl. Add the fish sauce, sugar, cornflour, chopped coriander, French beans and three tablespoons of breadcrumbs, and mix well.

Shape the mixture into cakes (patties) about two inches in diameter and a quarter inch thick. Roll in breadcrumbs.

Heat plenty of oil in a non-stick wok and deep-fry the fish cakes, a few at a time, for four to five minutes. Drain on absorbent paper.

Serve hot with the cucumber relish.

fried golden bags

20 (four-inch square) Wonton Wrappers (page no 94)

20 thin stalks spring onion greens

Oil for deep-frying

Stuffing

½ cup shredded raw crab meat

5-6 medium prawns, peeled, deveined and chopped

5-6 garlic cloves, chopped

1 tablespoon chopped fresh coriander leaves

5-6 black peppercorns, crushed

Salt to taste

1 spring onion, chopped

½ green chilli, chopped

½ tablespoon dark soy sauce

½ tablespoon fish sauce

Mix together all the ingredients for the stuffing in a bowl.

Spread out the wonton squares on a flat surface; place equal quantities of the crab meat stuffing in the centre of each wonton.

Pull the four corners up into the middle to make little bags.

Secure the bags around the middle with the spring onion greens. Be careful that the greens do not break while tying.

Heat the oil in a non-stick wok. Deep-fry the wonton bags till golden brown and crisp. Drain on absorbent paper.

Serve hot with chilli sauce.

Chef's Tip

Dip the spring onion greens in warm water to make them more pliable.

fried prawn balls

150 grams prawns, peeled

4 tablespoons Vegetable Stock (page 93)

1 tablespoon sake

1½ tablespoons cornflour

¼ teaspoon salt

Oil for deep-frying

To Serve

1½ tablespoons sea salt

½ teaspoon black pepper powder

½ lemon, cut into 4 wedges

Place the prawns, vegetable stock, sake, cornflour and salt in a food processor and process until smooth. Transfer the mixture into a small bowl.

Heat sufficient oil in a non-stick wok.

Grease a tablespoon and scoop two tablespoons of the prawn mixture and shape into a ball. Gently lower the ball into the hot oil and deep-fry till lightly browned. Drain and place on a wire rack. Repeat this process till all the mixture is used up.

Mix salt and black pepper powder in a small plate. Serve the fried prawn balls hot, garnished with lemon wedges and pepper-salt mixture.

quick canapés

4 slices brown bread

½ cup creamed butter/Mayonnaise (page 92)

2 eggs, boiled and sliced

2 tablespoons tomato ketchup

A few sprigs of fresh parsley

8-12 asparagus spears, trimmed, blanched and drained

1 teaspoon red chilli powder

½ small red capsicum, cut into ½-inch triangles

2 chicken sausages, sliced

¼ teaspoon chives

¼ cup American sweetcorn kernels

½ small cucumber, peeled and finely chopped

½ small green unripe mango, peeled and finely chopped

½ small onion, peeled and finely chopped

1 small tomato, finely chopped

Salt to taste

¼ teaspoon black pepper powder

½ small yellow capsicum, cut into ½ -inch triangles

½ small green capsicum, cut into ½ -inch triangles

¼ cup grated cheese

1 tablespoon lemon juice

A few sprigs of fresh mint leaves

Cut the brown bread slices into triangles or circles. Apply a little butter and toast them on a hot non-stick *tawa*.

Apply a little butter or mayonnaise on each canapé. Arrange the boiled egg slices on some canapés. Place a drop of tomato ketchup or butter over the egg. Top with a sprig of parsley and serve.

Cut the asparagus to the size of the base and place on some canapés. Pipe a dollop of butter over and sprinkle a little chilli powder. Garnish with a red capsicum triangle.

Place a piece of asparagus and a slice of sausage on some canapés. Pipe butter and sprinkle with chilli powder and garnish with chives. Top with a piece of red capsicum.

Mix together the sweetcorn, cucumber, unripe mango, onion, tomato, salt and pepper powder, red, yellow and green capsicums and grated cheese.

Add the remaining tomato ketchup and lemon juice. Place the mixture on some canapés and garnish with fresh mint sprigs.

Chef's Tip

Canapés can also be made by using salt biscuits, cheese crackers and canapé cases as a base.

chicken makhmali kebab

4 (200 grams each) chicken breasts
4-6 green chillies, chopped
1 inch ginger, roughly chopped
5-6 garlic cloves, roughly chopped
2/3 cup yogurt
¼ cup grated processed cheese
¼ cup fresh cream
½ teaspoon nutmeg powder
2 teaspoons *garam masala* powder
1 tablespoon honey
½ tablespoon lemon juice
Salt to taste
¼ cup butter

Chef's Tip
Use supremes of chicken for tender succulent kababs.

Remove the skin and bone and cut each chicken breast into two. Grind together the green chillies, ginger and garlic into a smooth paste. Rub the paste into the chicken, cover and set aside for fifteen minutes. Tie the yogurt up in a piece of muslin and set aside for half an hour to drain.

In a bowl, whisk together the drained yogurt, cheese, cream, nutmeg powder, *garam masala* powder, honey, lemon juice and salt to taste. Marinate the chicken in this mixture for three hours in a refrigerator. Place the chicken pieces, an inch apart, on a wire rack.

Cook the chicken in a Grill TOP and BOTTOM for twenty minutes, brushing with butter every five minutes. Serve hot with chutney.

kali mirch tikka

12-15 black peppercorns

500 grams boneless chicken, cut into ½-inch cubes

1 inch ginger

6-8 garlic cloves

2-3 green chillies

4 tablespoons oil

4 medium onions, sliced

1 cup drained (hung) yogurt

3 tablespoons fresh cream

1 tablespoon cornflour

1 egg white

½ teaspoon *garam masala* powder

1 medium green capsicum, cut into 1-inch pieces

Salt to taste

¼ teaspoon green cardamom powder

Butter for basting

Dry-roast the peppercorns and crush to a coarse powder. Grind the ginger, garlic and green chillies to a fine paste.

Heat the oil in a non-stick *kadai* and sauté the onions till brown. Cool and grind to a paste.

In a large bowl, combine the browned onion paste, yogurt, cream, cornflour, egg white, ginger-garlic-green chilli paste, *garam masala* powder, capsicum, crushed peppercorns, salt and cardamom powder.

Add the chicken cubes, mix well and set aside to marinate for one hour, preferably in a refrigerator.

Preheat the oven to 180^0C/350^0F/Gas Mark 4.

Thread the chicken cubes and capsicum cubes alternately on a skewer and cook in the preheated oven at 240^0C/475^0F/Gas Mark 9 for fifteen minutes, basting occasionally with butter.

Serve hot with onion rings and Mint Chutney (see below).

Mint Chutney

Grind 5 cups mint leaves, 3 cups coriander leaves, 10 green chillies, 3 onions, and 3 inches of ginger to a fine paste, adding a little water if required. Stir in 1 tablespoon lemon juice, salt and pomegranate seed powder to taste.

cheese balls

3 cups cheese spread
¾ cup refined flour
A pinch of salt
75 grams butter
3 eggs
2 teaspoons red chilli flakes
2 teaspoons mixed dried herbs
10-12 black peppercorns, crushed

Preheat an oven to 200°C/400°F/Gas Mark 6. Sift the flour with salt.

Place the butter and one cup of water in a non-stick pan and stir over low heat until the butter melts. Add the flour all at once and stir over medium heat until the mixture forms a ball and leaves the sides of the pan. Transfer the mixture to a bowl and cool slightly. Beat in the eggs, one at a time, until the mixture is smooth and shiny.

Spoon the mixture into a pastry bag fitted with a plain nozzle. Pipe small mounds onto a baking tray. Bake for twenty to twenty-five minutes or until puffed up and golden brown. Make a small hole in the base of the puffs with the tip of a knife or a skewer to allow the steam to escape. Return the puffs to the oven and bake for two more minutes to dry out the insides. Remove from the oven and set aside to cool.

Combine the cheese spread, chilli flakes, herbs and crushed peppercorns and mix well. Spoon into a small pastry bag with a plain nozzle and pipe the cheese mixture into the puffs through the hole in the base. Serve immediately.

Murgh ke shami

600 grams minced chicken
5 tablespoons split Bengal gram
2 inches ginger, finely chopped
10 garlic cloves, finely chopped
2 medium onions, chopped
1½ tablespoons chopped fresh coriander
1½ tablespoons chopped mint leaves
2 teaspoons lemon juice
2 tablespoons oil + for shallow-frying
½ teaspoon cumin seeds
½ teaspoon coriander seeds
5-6 black peppercorns
3-4 black cardamoms
2 teaspoons red chilli powder
½ teaspoon *garam masala* powder
½ teaspoon mace-cardamom powder
Salt to taste

Wash the minced chicken and drain out excess moisture. Soak the split gram for at least three hours.

Mix together the onions, chopped coriander and mint and lemon juice to make a stuffing. Divide into sixteen equal portions and set aside.

Heat two tablespoons of oil in a non-stick pan and add the cumin seeds, coriander seeds, peppercorns and black cardamoms; stir-fry for half a minute on medium heat. Add the chopped ginger, garlic and chilli powder.

Add the minced chicken and gram. Add two cups of water and bring to a boil. Reduce heat and cook, covered, till the gram is completely cooked. Cook on high heat to dry out the mixture completely, stirring continuously. Remove from heat and set aside to cool. Grind the chicken and gram mixture to a smooth paste. Add the *garam masala* powder, mace-cardamom powder and salt.

Mix well and check the seasoning. Divide into sixteen equal portions. Flatten each portion on the palm of your hand and place a portion of the onion stuffing in the centre. Shape into rounds and flatten slightly.

Heat the oil in a non-stick frying pan and shallow-fry till golden brown. Serve hot with onion *lachcha* and Mint Chutney (page 72).

Chef's Tip

If the chicken mixture is too moist after cooking, add roasted gram flour or powdered roasted split Bengal gram.

chicken lollipops

24 whole chicken wings
1 teaspoon garlic paste
2 teaspoons red chilli paste
1 teaspoon light soy sauce
1 teaspoon white vinegar
½ teaspoon white pepper powder
¼ teaspoon MSG (optional)
Salt to taste
¾ cup refined flour
¾ cup cornflour
2 eggs
6 tablespoons oil + for deep-frying

Clean and wash the chicken wings. Cut off the wing tips, remove the thin bone and pull the flesh to one end of the thick bone to make a 'lollipop'. Make a marinade of garlic paste, one teaspoon red chilli paste, soy sauce, vinegar, white pepper powder, MSG and salt. Marinate the chicken wings in this mixture for two hours, preferably in the refrigerator.

Meanwhile, mix together the refined flour, cornflour, eggs, six tablespoons of oil, remaining red chilli paste and salt to taste. Whisk thoroughly, with some water if required, to make a thick batter of pouring consistency. Rest the batter for fifteen to twenty minutes. Heat oil in a non-stick wok; dip the marinated wings in the batter and deep-fry on moderate heat, turning them over frequently, for three to four minutes, or until crisp and golden brown. Drain on absorbent paper. Serve hot with Sichuan Sauce (page 92).

til jhinga

24 (250 grams) medium prawns

1/3 cup sesame seeds

1 teaspoon garlic paste

1 teaspoon ginger paste

¼ teaspoon white pepper powder

Salt to taste

2 tablespoons lemon juice

2 tablespoons drained (hung) yogurt

½ cup grated processed cheese

½ teaspoon carom seeds

2 tablespoons cream

½ teaspoon mace-cardamom powder

1½ tablespoons powdered roasted split Bengal gram

1 cup breadcrumbs

Oil for deep-frying

Peel and devein the prawns, leaving the tails intact. Pat the prawns dry.

Mix together the garlic paste, ginger paste, white pepper powder, salt and lemon juice. Rub the paste all over the prawns and set aside for half an hour. Squeeze the prawns lightly to remove excess moisture and set aside.

Whisk together the drained yogurt and cheese till smooth. Add the carom seeds, cream, mace-cardamom powder and powdered roasted split Bengal gram. Coat the prawns with the mixture and set aside for half an hour.

Mix the breadcrumbs and sesame seeds on a plate. Roll the prawns in the mixture and refrigerate for about fifteen minutes.

Heat the oil in a non-stick *kadai* and deep-fry the prawns over medium heat for about four or five minutes. Drain and set aside for four or five minutes.

Deep-fry again for two or three minutes. Drain on absorbent paper.

Serve hot with lemon wedges and Green Chutney (page 14).

chao tom
(prawns on sugarcane sticks)

8 six-inch long sugarcane sticks, peeled

2 tablespoons oil

1 tablespoon roasted rice powder

¼ teaspoon black pepper powder

Seasoned Prawns

300 grams medium prawns, peeled and deveined

1 teaspoon salt

¼ cup minced chicken

¼ cup flaked white fish fillet

3 garlic cloves

3 shallots

1 teaspoon sugar

1 egg white, beaten

1 tablespoon fish sauce

Garnish

1 head iceberg lettuce, leaves separated

80 grams rice vermicelli (optional), blanched and drained

4 shallots, sliced and crisply fried

A few sprigs of fresh coriander

A few sprigs of fresh mint

To Serve

Fish Sauce Dip (page 91)

For the seasoned prawns, rub salt into the prawns and set aside for fifteen minutes. Rinse and drain.

Grind the prawns, chicken, fish, garlic, shallots and sugar to a paste in a blender. Add the egg white, fish sauce, roasted rice powder and pepper powder, and mix well. Divide into eight equal portions.

Lightly grease your hands and wrap a portion of the prawn mixture tightly around the middle of a sugarcane stick. Repeat with the remaining mixture and sugarcane sticks.

Heat a non-stick grill pan and grill the sticks over medium heat for five to ten minutes, rotating them frequently, until lightly browned on all sides. Remove and place on a plate.

On individual serving plates, arrange the lettuce leaves, rice vermicelli, fried shallots, coriander and mint. Arrange the prawn sticks on top and serve with the fish sauce dip.

keema potli

400 grams minced mutton
1 cup refined flour
2 tablespoons semolina
Salt to taste
¼ cup ghee
2 tablespoons oil + for deep-frying
1 teaspoon cumin seeds
2 inches fresh ginger, chopped
3 green chillies, chopped
1 teaspoon red chilli powder
1 tablespoon coriander powder
1 teaspoon cumin powder
¾ cup yogurt
1 teaspoon *garam masala* powder
A few sprigs of fresh coriander, chopped

Knead together the flour, semolina, salt and ghee with enough warm water to make a stiff dough. Keep covered for thirty minutes. Divide the dough into twenty balls.

Heat two tablespoons of oil in a non-stick *kadai* and add cumin seeds. When they change colour, add the *keema* and sauté till half-cooked. Add half a cup of water if required.

Add the chopped ginger, green chillies, chilli powder, coriander powder, cumin powder and salt. Mix well. Cover and cook on low heat for fifteen minutes.

Stir in the yogurt and cook on high heat for ten minutes, stirring continuously. Cook till the *keema* is completely cooked and dry.

Sprinkle the *garam masala* powder and chopped coriander and mix well. Cool. Divide into twenty portions.

Roll the balls of dough into three-inch round *puri*. Place a portion of the *keema* in the centre. Apply a little water a little away from the edges of the *puri*, gather the edges together in the shape of a *potli* or *modak*. Pinch the folds together to seal.

Heat sufficient oil in a non-stick *kadai*. Deep-fry the *potli* in moderately hot oil till golden brown. Serve with a chutney of your choice.

salsa fresca

4 medium tomatoes

1 medium onion, chopped finely

2 jalapeño chilliies, chopped finely

Juice of ½ lemon

2 teaspoons olive oil

1 teaspoon vinegar

½ teaspoon salt

½ teaspoon dried oregano, crushed

¼ cup fresh coriander, roughly chopped

Make a cross slit on the bottom of each tomato and immerse in boiling water for half a minute.

Drain the tomatoes, peel, remove the seeds and chop roughly.

In a medium bowl, combine the tomatoes, onion and chilli.

Add the olive oil, vinegar, lemon juice and salt. Add the crushed oregano.

Mix well and let the sauce stand for at least two hours for the flavours to mingle.

Stir in the chopped coriander. Serve at room temperature with nachos or crisps.

thousand island dip

1 cup Mayonnaise (page 92)

1 medium pickled gherkin, chopped

2 small shallots, chopped

2 tablespoons tomato ketchup

1 teaspoon Tabasco sauce

1 tablespoon lemon juice

Salt to taste

3-4 black peppercorns, crushed

2 tablespoons fresh parsley, chopped

Add the gherkins, shallots and tomato ketchup to the mayonnaise and mix well.

Add the Tabasco sauce, lemon juice, salt and crushed peppercorns. Mix well with a wooden spoon.

Check the seasoning, and add the parsley.

Transfer the dip to a bowl, cover and chill in the refrigerator.

Serve chilled, with wafers or pieces of fresh vegetable (crudités).

roasted capsicum and tomato dip

1 medium red capsicum, seeded and quartered

5 medium tomatoes, seeded and quartered

5-6 garlic cloves

Salt to taste

2 teaspoons sugar

2 tablespoons lemon juice

Fresh parsley sprig, for garnishing

Preheat an oven to 180^{0}C/350^{0}F/Gas Mark 4.

Arrange the red capsicum and tomato quarters along with the garlic in a baking tray. Sprinkle salt over them.

Roast in the oven for twenty to twenty-five minutes. Remove from the oven and cool. Peel the capsicum, tomatoes and garlic, and chop finely.

Heat a non-stick pan and roast the garlic for a minute. Add the capsicum and tomatoes and cook for two minutes. Add the salt and sugar. Mix well.

Cook for another two minutes and add lemon juice. Mix again. Serve, garnished with a sprig of parsley.

crudités with herbed paneer and yogurt dip

1 large carrot, cut into 2-inch fingers

1 large cucumber, cut into 2-inch fingers

6-8 pieces of baby corn, blanched

1 small radish, cut into 2-inch fingers

2 medium tomatoes, quartered

Dip

¾ cup cottage cheese, grated

¾ cup drained (hung) yogurt

1 tablespoon chopped fresh parsley

Salt to taste

½ tablespoon olive oil

1 tablespoon chopped burnt garlic

Chef's Tip

To prepare the burnt garlic, fry two tablespoons of chopped garlic in three to four tablespoons of oil till light golden brown. Drain immediately.

Arrange the cut vegetables on a serving platter and place in a refrigerator to chill.

For the dip, process the cottage cheese, yogurt, parsley and salt in a blender for two minutes till smooth.

Transfer the mixture to a serving bowl. Pour the olive oil over and sprinkle with the burnt garlic

Serve with the chilled crudités (raw vegetable fingers).

avocado dip

1 medium avocado

1 small onion, chopped

¼ cup fresh coriander, chopped

1 medium green capsicum, chopped

Salt to taste

4 medium tomatoes, chopped

Cut the avocado in half and remove the stone. Process half the onion, half the fresh coriander, the capsicum and salt to a smooth paste. Scoop out the flesh of the remaining half avocado and mash roughly with the paste. Add the tomatoes, remaining onion and fresh coriander. Mix well and serve immediately with nachos, crackers or crudités (cut raw vegetables).

peanut yogurt dip

2 cups drained (hung) yogurt

¼ cup peanuts, roasted and crushed coarsely

2 tablespoons fresh coriander, chopped

2 whole red chillies, crushed

Salt to taste

¼ cup cream

Place the yogurt in a mixing bowl; whisk to get a smooth texture. Season with salt, add the crushed red chillies and peanuts and chopped coriander. Whisk in the cream and mix well.

cheese and herb dip

1 cup grated cheese
¼ teaspoon dried oregano
¼ teaspoon dried thyme
¼ cup milk
Salt to taste
¼ cup white pepper powder

Mix together the cheese and milk. Heat the mixture in a double boiler or in a heatproof bowl placed over a pan of simmering water till the cheese melts and the mixture gets a smooth consistency. Season with salt, pepper and dried herbs. Serve immediately or it will thicken again.

saucy tomato dip

6 medium tomatoes, chopped
2 shallots, chopped
3 garlic cloves, peeled and chopped
3 green chillies, finely chopped
2 tablespoons olive oil
Salt to taste
8-10 black peppercorns, crushed
10 fresh basil leaves, roughly torn

Place the tomatoes in a large bowl. Add the shallots, garlic and green chillies and mix well. Add the olive oil, salt and crushed peppercorns. Mix with a wooden spoon and grind coarsely. Check the seasoning and add roughly torn basil leaves.

melting cheese dip

1½ cups grated processed cheese

½ cup milk

1 tablespoon tinned jalapeños, drained and chopped

Salt to taste

½ teaspoon Tabasco sauce

1 tablespoon fresh coriander, chopped

Heat the milk in a double boiler. Gradually add the cheese and cook, stirring continuously, till smooth. Stir in the jalapeños, salt and Tabasco sauce. Remove from heat, add the chopped coriander and stir well. Serve immediately with nachos or wafers.

fish sauce dip

2-3 fresh red chillies, seeded and sliced

3 cloves garlic

¼ cup sugar

3 tablespoons lemon juice

1 tablespoon vinegar

3 tablespoons fish sauce

Salt to taste

To make the fish sauce dip, grind the chillies and garlic coarsely. Add the rest of the ingredients and stir until the sugar dissolves.

basic recipes

Mayonnaise

Place 1 egg yolk, salt to taste, ¼ teaspoon each white pepper powder, French mustard and sugar and 1 teaspoon vinegar in a clean bowl and mix thoroughly with a whisk. Alternatively, process the mixture in a blender. Add 1 cup of oil, a little at a time, whisking or blending continuously, until all the oil is incorporated. Add 1 teaspoon lemon juice and adjust seasoning. Store in an airtight jar in a refrigerator.

Red Curry Paste

Pound together 10 dried, seeded, soaked and drained long red chillies, a large pinch of salt, 1½ tablespoons chopped galangal, 3 tablespoons chopped lemon grass, 2 teaspoons grated kaffir lime rind, 1 tablespoon chopped fresh coriander roots, 1 tablespoon chopped red shallots and 2 tablespoons chopped garlic with a pestle and mortar, to a smooth paste. Alternatively grind all the ingredients together in a grinder till smooth.

Makes half a cup of curry paste.

Sichuan Sauce

Boil 10-12 dried red chillies in 1 cup of water for 5 to 7 minutes. Drain, cool and grind to a fine paste. Heat ½ cup oil in a pan; add 10 finely chopped garlic cloves, 2 finely chopped green chillies, 2 finely chopped spring onions and 1 inch ginger, grated, and sauté for 1 minute. Add the red chilli paste and sauté for a few more seconds. Add 2-3 inches celery stalk, finely chopped, 3 tablespoons tomato ketchup and salt to taste, and stir well to mix. Stir in 2 teaspoons white vinegar and simmer for 1 minute till the oil rises to the surface. Cool and store.

Note: Sichuan sauce will keep for 1 month if there is sufficient oil covering the surface.

Vegetable Stock

Peel, wash and chop 1 onion, ½ medium carrot, 2-3 inch celery stalk and 2-3 garlic cloves. Place in a pan with 1 bay leaf, 5-6 peppercorns, 2-3 cloves and 5 cups of water and bring to a boil. Lower heat and simmer for 15 minutes and strain. Cool and store in a refrigerator till further use.

White Sauce

Melt 1½ tablespoons of butter in a thick-bottomed pan. Add 1½ tablespoons refined flour; stir and cook the roux (butter-flour mixture) over low heat with a wooden spoon. When it develops a sandy texture, remove from heat and cool. Peel 1 onion. Wrap a bay leaf around it studding it with 2 cloves at the two ends. Bring 1½ cups milk to a boil with the onion. Remove the onion. Pour the boiling hot milk into the cold roux, stirring continuously, to prevent lumps from forming. Simmer gently for 2 minutes. Add a small pinch of nutmeg and season with salt to taste and ¼ teaspoon white pepper powder. Melt ½ tablespoon butter and gently pour over the top of the sauce to prevent a skin forming.

Variations:

1. **Cream sauce:** Add ¼ cup of cream and 2 tablespoons of melted butter to the white sauce.

2. **Parsley sauce:** Add 1 tablespoon of chopped parsley to the cream sauce.

Wonton Wrappers

Knead 2 cups of refined flour with ½ cup warm water to make a firm dough. Roll the dough into a large thin square sheet, about 1 mm thick. Cut into 3-inch squares and use as required.

glossary

English	Hindi
Almonds	Badam
Asafoetida	Hing
Asparagus	Shatavari
Avocado	Makkhan phal
Basil	Tulsi
Bay leaf	Tej patta
Bean sprouts	Ankurit moong
Bengal gram, split, roasted	Daalia
Bengal gram, slpit	Chana dal
Black gram, skinless, split	Dhuli urad dal
Black peppercorns	Kali mirch
Capsicum	Shimla mirch
Caraway seeds	Shahi jeera
Cardamom, green	Chhoti elaichi
Cardamoms, black	Badi elaichi
Carom seeds	Ajwain
Chickpeas	Kabuli chana
Coriander seeds	Dhania
Corn kernels	Makai ke dane
Cottage cheese	Paneer
Cumin seeds	Jeera
Fennel seeds	Badi Saunf
Fenugreek leaves, dried	Kasoori methi
Fenugreek seeds	Methi dana
French beans	Farsi
Gram flour	Besan
Green gram, skinless split	Dhuli moong dal

English	Hindi	English	Hindi
Jaggery	Gur	Prawns	Jhinga
Lettuce leaves	Salad ke patte	Radish	Mooli
Lotus roots	Bhein	Raisins	Kishmish
Mace	Javitri	Refined flour	Maida
Maize flour	Makai ka atta	Rice, parboiled	Ukda chawal
Mango, unripe, green	Keri	Sago	Sabudana
Mint	Pudina	Semolina	Sooji/rawa
Mushroom	Khumb	Sesame seeds	Til
Mustard seeds	Rai	Shallots	Chhote pyaaz
Nutmeg	Jaiphal	Spring onion greens	Hare pyaaz ki pattiyan
Olive	Jaitun	Sugarcane	Ganna
Parsley	Ajmoda	Tamarind	Imli
Peanuts	Moongphalli	Vinegar	Sirka
Pigeon peas, split	Arhar dal/toovar dal	Walnut	Akhrot
Pineapple	Annanas	Yogurt	Dahi
Pomegranate kernels	Anar ke dane		